Original title:
The Snowy Veil

Copyright © 2024 Swan Charm
All rights reserved.

Author: Olivia Orav
ISBN HARDBACK: 978-9908-52-047-6
ISBN PAPERBACK: 978-9908-52-048-3
ISBN EBOOK: 978-9908-52-049-0

Tales of a Frosted Horizon

On the edge of winter's breath,
The sun dips low in muted light.
Whispers dance in icy air,
As shadows stretch, embracing night.

Frozen tales on frosted ground,
Each crystal spark a story spun.
Nature's canvas, white and round,
Awakens dreams that softly run.

Beneath the blanket, silence sings,
A symphony of quiet grace.
In the chill, a warmth still clings,
As time slows down to find its place.

Stars ignite the velvet sky,
A glittering array above.
Each twinkle holds a distant sigh,
And whispers of the heart's pure love.

With footsteps soft on snow-kissed land,
Adventures wait in every glance.
The world, a frozen wonderland,
Inviting all to take a chance.

Snowbound Haven of Solitude

In the stillness, time drifts slow,
A single flake begins its fall.
In this haven, peace will grow,
As winter weaves its quiet call.

Blankets white across the floor,
Echoes of a soft embrace.
Behind each closed and quiet door,
Lies warmth found in this sacred space.

The fire crackles, shadows play,
As candles flicker with their glow.
In this gentle light, we stay,
And let our worries melt like snow.

Lonely whispers fill the air,
As thoughts unspool like winter dreams.
In every corner, joys we share,
And laughter dances through the beams.

Solitude, a friend so dear,
In snowbound realms, we find our way.
With every heartbeat, crystal clear,
Winter's breath brings peace to stay.

Whispers of Frosted Dreams

In twilight's hush, the whispers flow,
Where dreams wrapped tight in frost do glow.
Stars twinkle soft, the night unveiled,
As silent thoughts of warmth prevailed.

Beneath the moon's ethereal light,
The frost-kissed air ignites the night.
In every breath, a tale concealed,
Of hopes and wishes gently healed.

Shimmering Silence

Amidst the stillness, crystals gleam,
In twilight's grasp, the world will dream.
Each flake a whisper, soft and bright,
In shimmering silence, pure delight.

The frozen air breathes tales untold,
Of winter's touch, both fierce and bold.
Nature holds its breath in grace,
A tranquil peace, a warm embrace.

Frost's Gentle Caress

A touch so light upon the ground,
Frost's gentle caress, magic found.
It weaves a spell with every breath,
As nature whispers tales of death.

But life awakes in colors bright,
Amidst the chill of winter's night.
The world transformed, a canvas new,
In frosted glimmers, dreams break through.

Veils of Winter's Embrace

Veils of white in silence lay,
A cover soft where shadows play.
Between the trees, the echoes hum,
Winter's embrace, a song unsung.

The world adorned in icy lace,
Time stands still in this frozen space.
Each step a breath, a dance so fine,
In winter's arms, our hearts align.

Whispers of the Winter Air

The snowflakes dance and twirl,
As soft whispers fill the night.
They wrap the world in silence,
A sparkling, soft delight.

Beneath the moon's pale glow,
Footprints trace a fleeting path.
Each breath a misty secret,
In winter's gentle bath.

The trees are draped in crystal,
With branches bowed and low.
Each sigh of wind a story,
In whispers soft and slow.

Starry skies gleam bright above,
In the calm of winter's charm.
A world that holds its secret,
In nature's tender arm.

Through the realms of winter air,
Life pauses, takes a breath.
In the stillness of this moment,
We find our thoughts of depth.

Glacial Memories Unfurled

Icebergs drift on tranquil seas,
While echoes of the past unfold.
Stories carved in frozen waves,
In glacial blue and gold.

The valleys hold her whispers,
Silent tales of yesteryears.
Each layer speaks of seasons,
Of laughter mixed with tears.

In the distance, mountains rise,
Guardians of the wintry land.
They cradle ancient secrets,
With grace, both bold and grand.

Winds carry scents of pine,
Through the crisp and airy night.
Each breath a sweet reminder,
Of memories, pure and bright.

As the sun begins to set,
Shadows stretch across the ice.
In this realm of glacial dreams,
We find our hearts precise.

Enfolded in a Winter's Embrace

Wrapped in layers rich and warm,
We gather by the fire's glow.
Outside the world is slumbering,
In blankets soft with snow.

Laughter echoes in the air,
As stories dance from tongue to tongue.
Each moment shared a treasure,
A melody sweetly sung.

The frost adorns the windowpanes,
Like lace upon a silk thread.
In winter's gentle embrace,
We lay our dreams to bed.

Softly falling snowflakes weave,
A tapestry of white delight.
In the hush of this stillness,
Our hearts are filled with light.

Together through the winters,
We find a warmth so true.
In the glow of cozy moments,
Life's beauty shines anew.

Pondering Paths Through a Whitened World

The paths ahead are blanketed,
In white, untouched and bright.
Each way a new beginning,
Inviting us to take flight.

Footprints mark the journey,
Underneath the frost-kissed trees.
With every step, we wander,
Through the chill of winter's breeze.

The laughter of the children,
Echoes in the snowy air.
Each moment is an adventure,
A season rich and rare.

As shadows lengthen softly,
The day begins to wane.
In the glow of twilight's charm,
Our hearts sing out again.

Searching for the paths of grace,
In this world of white anew.
We ponder every journey,
And the wonders we pursue.

Enveloping the Stillness

In the hush of the night,
Soft whispers drift and flow.
Gentle shadows embrace,
As the world ebbs low.

Moonlight spills like silk,
On the still, frozen ground.
Time seems to pause here,
In silence, we're found.

Stars twinkle above,
A distant, lucid gaze.
Each breath a soft echo,
In tranquil, wintry haze.

The air is crisp and clear,
With a hint of frosty breath.
Nature holds its secrets,
In this calm, quiet depth.

In moments like these,
Our worries fade away.
Enveloped in stillness,
We find peace in the gray.

Dancing in the White

Snowflakes twirl and glide,
As winter's joy unfolds.
Children laugh and giggle,
In the white, they mold.

Footprints mark the path,
Of stories yet untold.
With every leap and bound,
Magic starts to hold.

The trees draped in white,
Stand like guardians tall.
With arms open wide,
They catch each snowy fall.

A world dressed in shimmer,
With sparkles all around.
Nature's joyful ballet,
In silence, it is found.

As day turns into dusk,
The sky paints its own art.
Dancing in the white,
Fills every heart.

Shards of Ice

Glistening on branches,
In the morning's pale light.
Each shard tells a story,
Of winter's pure might.

The world, a crystal scene,
Where silence reigns supreme.
Nature's frozen canvas,
A shimmering dream.

Underneath the surface,
Rivers hide and flow.
Beneath icy diamonds,
Life continues to grow.

The sun's warm caress,
Creates prisms in the air.
Shards of ice begin melting,
As they whisper, beware.

In this fleeting moment,
We savor the bright spell.
For shards of ice remind us,
Of the stories we tell.

Dreams of Light

In twilight's embrace,
Whispers of dawn begin.
Dreams of light awaken,
As the day draws in.

Stars twinkle above,
In the velvety sky.
Each one holds a wish,
As night drifts by.

Moonshine bathes the earth,
In its gentle hold.
Dreams spin like silver,
In the night, unfold.

Awake in the darkness,
Possibilities bloom.
With every soft heartbeat,
Hope chases the gloom.

As morning approaches,
With colors that ignite.
We dance in the shadows,
Chasing dreams of light.

When Winter Wears its Best

In the splendor of frost,
Everything seems renewed.
Nature dons its white robe,
All is serene and hued.

The air is crisp and clear,
Filled with magical cheer.
When winter wears its best,
The world feels so near.

With every flake that falls,
A masterpiece is made.
Whispers curl like smoke,
In the stillness, we wade.

Trees stand proud and tall,
Draped in a glistening coat.
In this quiet grandeur,
Our hearts learn to float.

When the cold bites our cheeks,
Yet warmth fills our soul.
As winter wears its best,
We find ourselves whole.

Enigma Wrapped in White

Snowflakes dance in silent flight,
Veiling earth in purest light.
Whispers soft upon the breeze,
Nature's hush, a gentle tease.

Shadows blend with winter's song,
In this world where dreams belong.
Mysteries in every flake,
A hidden truth, a fragile wake.

Footprints lost in drifts unseen,
Paths obscured where we have been.
Secrets cradled, tightly wound,
In the silence, wonders found.

Scattered stars, the night's embrace,
Softly draping, time and space.
Like a shroud, the purest white,
Wraps the world in quiet night.

A canvas vast, untouched ground,
Life resumes without a sound.
In the stillness, we confide,
Enigma wrapped, we abide.

Chilling Caress of Stillness

Frosty air with breath of night,
Holds the whisper of pure light.
Branches laden, quiet grace,
Nature sighs in frozen space.

In the still, the heart can hear,
Echoed thoughts that draw us near.
Every flake a story told,
Of silent wonders, brave and bold.

Moonlight paints the world in white,
Casting spells with gentle light.
Chilling caress upon the skin,
Awakens dreams that lie within.

Footfalls muffled, lost in time,
In this realm of snow and rhyme.
Stillness reigns, a soothing balm,
In the frost, we find our calm.

As shadows stretch and fade away,
Morning greets the break of day.
With open arms, the world awaits,
In the stillness, love resonates.

Echoes of the Snowfall

Gentle whispers in the air,
Snowflakes falling everywhere.
With each flake, a story swells,
In the silence, magic dwells.

Softly blanketing the ground,
Nature's peace, a soothing sound.
Every flurry, time stands still,
Echoes weave with tender thrill.

Moonlit paths all shimmer white,
A tranquil scene, a pure delight.
Through the woods, the shadows play,
Guided softly by the gray.

Memories etched in frozen time,
Every echo, every chime.
Voices of the past resound,
In this stillness, hope is found.

In the depth of winter's night,
Stars emerge as twinkling light.
Whispers fade to softly call,
Embrace the echoes of the fall.

Pale Reflections in Winter's Gleam

In winter's grasp, the world seems still,
Covered deep by nature's thrill.
Pale reflections, crystal bright,
Dance under the pale moonlight.

Silvery shadows glide and weave,
Secrets of the night believe.
Frosted branches, light's embrace,
Whisper tales of time and space.

The icy breath, a gentle sigh,
Painting stories as they fly.
In stillness lies a tranquil dream,
Capturing the softest gleam.

Each snowflake, a fleeting dance,
In this world, we find our chance.
To wander far in blushing white,
Through winter's heart, beneath its light.

In glistening peace, we draw near,
To the beauty, ever clear.
Pale reflections hold the key,
To the wonders of the sea.

Tranquil Slumber Under Snow

Soft whispers of night call,
Blankets of white embrace all.
Stars twinkle gently above,
Wrapping the world in sweet love.

Silent dreams drift and sway,
In winter's soft, hushed ballet.
Hushed voices of the trees,
Swaying gently in the breeze.

Moonlight kisses the ground,
While peace and calm abound.
Nature rests without a sound,
In this serene, sacred mound.

A palette of dreams and sighs,
Where imagination flies.
In the stillness, hearts glow,
Finding warmth under the snow.

Enchanted Fields of Ice

Fields stretch wide, gleaming bright,
Nature's wonders bathed in light.
Crystals shimmer, a magical sight,
In this realm of frosty delight.

Every breath, a misty cloud,
Silence sings, both soft and loud.
With each step, the heart beats proud,
Lost in dreams, wrapped in a shroud.

Whispers echo through the night,
Caressed by the moon's soft light.
In a world where time takes flight,
Everything feels just right.

Frozen petals, unique and rare,
Adorn the ground with utmost care.
In this place, magic fills the air,
Every moment beyond compare.

Muffled Footsteps on Frozen Ground

Soft footsteps crunch and glide,
Through the beauty winter hides.
Echoes dance in chilly air,
Trace the paths that lead nowhere.

Silent shadows gently creep,
As the world is lost in sleep.
Memories carved in ice and snow,
Whispers of the past that flow.

With each step, a story told,
Of dreams and desires bold.
Captured in the frosty art,
Of winter's delightful heart.

Beneath the starlit canopy,
Footprints fade, yet memories free.
In this night, all spirits combine,
In the frozen, woven line.

Snowflakes Dance in the Moonlight

Snowflakes twirl, a graceful dance,
In the moon's enchanting trance.
Spinning down, a diamond's song,
In their flight, where they belong.

Glistening like jewels on trees,
Whispers carried by the breeze.
Each flake unique, a work of art,
Bringing magic to the heart.

Twilight shimmers, shadows play,
As the night turns into day.
Caught in joy, the world wears white,
Wrapped in warmth, pure and bright.

With every swirl, dreams ignited,
Layered joys, softly invited.
In the stillness, joy takes flight,
Snowflakes dance in the moonlight.

Fleeting Impressions of a Chill

A whisper of cold upon my skin,
Leaves dance and twirl in the wind.
Echoes of laughter fade away,
As shadows stretch through the gray.

The world dressed in silver and white,
Hiding warmth in the depths of night.
Footprints vanish, soft as a sigh,
Memories linger, then say goodbye.

Frosted breath in the morning air,
Nature prepares for the silent prayer.
In twinkling stars, secrets entwined,
A moment of peace, so rare to find.

The chill wraps close, a tender embrace,
In this frozen world, a gentle place.
A fleeting glance at what we know,
In whispers of chill, the feelings flow.

Every flake a story to tell,
Capturing warmth where we dwell.
In the quiet, we find our peace,
As fleeting impressions slowly cease.

Mirrors of Ice in the Shade

Glistening stillness, a world made clear,
Mirrors of ice begin to appear.
In every corner, nature's art,
Reflecting the wonder, a frozen heart.

The sunlight plays on shimmering glass,
Moments held tight, as seconds pass.
Beauty captured in the cool air,
Each glance a secret, a quiet prayer.

Shadows linger, soft and low,
In the stillness, feelings grow.
Echoes of whispers, soft and sweet,
As frozen paths where hearts may meet.

Time stands still in this frosty embrace,
With every sparkle, a quiet grace.
Nature's canvas, painted bright,
Mirrors of ice in the fading light.

In the silence, we hear the call,
Inviting us to share it all.
Reflections deep in the winter shade,
Where moments of magic are lovingly laid.

Unveiling Secrets of the Frosted Morning

As dawn breaks softly, secrets unfold,
A tapestry woven in silver and gold.
Each breath of frost tells a tale,
Of starry nights and winter's veil.

The world awakens, fresh and new,
With whispers of dreams that morning drew.
In the quiet, truths come alive,
In every sparkle, magic thrives.

Branches heavy with crystals gleam,
Holding the echoes of a wistful dream.
The chill in the air, an inviting tease,
In this frozen realm, hearts find their ease.

The sun ascends, a fiery glow,
As shadows retreat, soft and slow.
Secrets revealed in the light of day,
Where frost and warmth together play.

In frost-kissed beauty, we stand and see,
What nature unveils, wild and free.
A frosted morning, serene and bright,
Holds whispers of magic, pure delight.

Winter's Still Breath

In the hush of winter, breaths are still,
Nature holds secrets, a timeless thrill.
With every flake that graces the ground,
An orchestra plays without a sound.

Through branches bare, the cold winds sweep,
Like gentle lullabies, coaxing us to sleep.
The world draped in white, so peaceful and clear,
Whispers of winter, we hold dear.

Time seems frozen, as moments unfold,
In silence, the stories of winter are told.
Each crack and creak of the evening chill,
A reminder of magic that lingers still.

With the moon hanging low in velvet skies,
Winter's still breath lulls, as time gently flies.
Wrapped in warmth, we find our place,
Cocooned in the glow of night's embrace.

In the quietude, we pause to reflect,
On the beauty of life we often neglect.
Winter's still breath carries us near,
To the heart of the season we hold dear.

Glittering Frost on the Pines

Glistening frost on the pines,
Whispers secrets of the night,
Shimmering under moonlight,
Nature's jewels, pure and bright.

Each needle dressed in icy lace,
Beneath the stars, they softly sway,
In this still and quiet place,
Winter's breath keeps dreams at bay.

Footsteps crunch on frosted ground,
Echoes mingle with the breeze,
Magic waits, so profound,
Among the towering ice trees.

Morning sun will soon arise,
Kissing frost with gentle light,
Transforming all beneath the skies,
From silver white to warm and bright.

But for now, the cold remains,
A silken veil on nature's face,
In the woods, where peace contains,
Glittering frost in timeless grace.

Secrets of the Icebound Woods

In the icebound woods so deep,
Lies a world both dark and light,
Frozen still, where shadows creep,
Secrets hiding from our sight.

Moonlit paths of crystal glow,
Lead us to the silent glade,
Where the ancient willows bow,
And the night's calm serenade.

Whispers drift upon the chill,
Tales of winter's silent reign,
In the heart, a magic thrill,
The woods reveal their hidden grain.

Frozen streams weave silver threads,
Beneath the veil of frosted leaves,
Where the quiet wisdom spreads,
And the land in silence grieves.

Tread lightly on the snowy carpet,
Listen close to nature's heart,
In this realm, a secret market,
Where the past and present part.

Hushed Echoes Under Winter's Mantle

Under winter's soft embrace,
Hushed echoes find their way,
Through the white and silent space,
Where the world is cold and gray.

Snowflakes dance on gentle breeze,
Filling every crevice, nook,
Nature's song evokes a tease,
Pages turned in frozen book.

Crisp air carries whispers low,
Of the tales the winter weaves,
In the twinkling, falling snow,
Rests the memory of leaves.

Frosted branches arch with care,
Cradling secrets of the night,
In the stillness, all seems bare,
Yet within shines hidden light.

With each step, the crunch will sing,
Of the dreams beneath the frost,
In this world of muted spring,
Where the past's warm breath is lost.

Radiant White Haven

In a haven of radiant white,
Fresh snow blankets the earth's skin,
Soft as whispers in the night,
A new adventure to begin.

Mountains clad in winter's glow,
Stand tall against the azure sky,
As crystal rivers gently flow,
Reflecting dreams that never die.

Every tree, a story laced,
With the glow of frosty breath,
Charms of peace forever placed,
In this land where time is death.

Children's laughter fills the air,
Creating paths through fields of snow,
With each twirl, we leave a dare,
In the light where shadows glow.

At twilight's call, the world seems bright,
Under stars that softly shimmer,
In this haven of sheer delight,
Winter's magic will not dimmer.

Crystalline Serenity

In the stillness, whispers glide,
Snowflakes dance, in grace they hide.
A crystal world, so pure, so bright,
We breathe in peace, in soft twilight.

Trees adorned in shimmering white,
Guardian figures, cloaked in light.
Silence sings a sacred song,
In this realm, we all belong.

Footsteps crunch on blankets deep,
Secrets waiting, dreams to keep.
Every glance reveals a tale,
Where winter winds softly wail.

Guided by the moon's soft glow,
Hearts awake in chilling flow.
Moments frozen, time suspended,
In serene wonder, we are blended.

Within the silence, souls ignite,
Finding warmth in winter's bite.
A crystalline embrace we share,
In this beauty, we find care.

Frosted Thoughts in a Silent World

Thoughts wrapped in blankets of frost,
In the silence, what is lost?
Every breath a cloud of dreams,
In this stillness, nothing seems.

Whispers float on wintry air,
Echoes linger everywhere.
Each step prints a fleeting mark,
In the quiet, there's a spark.

Branches bow with laden grace,
Veils of snow, a soft embrace.
Time slows down, the heart aligns,
Finding peace in quiet signs.

Thoughts of warmth in bitter chill,
Winter murmurs, calm and still.
Frosted moments, rare and sweet,
In this world, our hearts compete.

In the stillness, stories weave,
Magic dwells in what we believe.
Frosted thoughts, a gentle guide,
In silence, our hopes abide.

Shimmering Echoes of Winter's Breath

Echoes shimmer, freeze in time,
Winter whispers, soft as rhyme.
In the distance, soft and clear,
A symphony of snow draws near.

Glistening paths beneath our feet,
Nature's canvas, pure and sweet.
Every corner, every sight,
Holds the magic of the night.

Breath suspended, held so tight,
Silhouettes in soft moonlight.
Crystals twinkle, bright and bold,
Tales of winter soon unfold.

Threads of silence gently weave,
In the pause, we dare believe.
Moments frozen, hearts entwined,
In the echo, peace we find.

Shimmering beauty, soft and bright,
In the chill of winter's bite.
Close your eyes and breathe it in,
Let the echoes guide you in.

The Lightness Beneath the Snow

Beneath the snow, the earth does sleep,
Hibernation, secrets keep.
Gentle rhythms pulse with life,
Silent moments free from strife.

Lightness dances through the chill,
Whispers weave, the heart can feel.
Each flake falls, a soft caress,
Nature's touch, a warm caress.

Underneath the icy veil,
Life renewing, soft and frail.
Roots that stretch and dreams that grow,
Invisible beneath the snow.

In the quiet, seeds await,
Spring's embrace, a lingering fate.
Soon the earth will wake and rise,
Beneath the warmth of sunny skies.

Life persists where stillness reigns,
In the frosty, gentle plains.
The lightness waits, a soft decree,
Beneath the snow, we yearn to be.

Echoes in the Flurry

Whispers dance upon the breeze,
Snowflakes swirl like gentle ease,
Footprints fade in the soft white,
Echoes linger, lost from sight.

Winter's breath, a soft caress,
Blankets wrap in stillness' dress,
Nature hushes, secrets shared,
In this realm, we roam unpaired.

A silent hymn sings through the night,
Branches shimmer, bathed in light,
Each flake tells a tale untold,
In the chill, our hearts unfold.

Frozen whispers, soft and shy,
Beneath the vast and starry sky,
Echoes of dreams drift and melt,
In this peace, our souls are felt.

As morn arrives, the world refreshed,
Hope and wonder, gently meshed,
In the flurry, life resumes,
Carried forth by winter's tunes.

An Elegy in White

A shroud of white envelops earth,
Veiling all with silent mirth,
Each flake a tear from skies above,
An elegy for what we love.

Barren branches stretch and sway,
Whispers of the past decay,
Memories in the frosty air,
In the stillness, thoughts laid bare.

Moonlight glistens on the frost,
In this moment, nothing's lost,
Each breath hangs in the night so stark,
A fleeting thought, a glowing spark.

As morning breaks, the silence wanes,
Life awakens, love remains,
Yet in shadows of the cold,
Echoes of our stories told.

An elegy in white we write,
For all we've lost, for every light,
In the snow, our hopes arise,
In the quiet, beneath pale skies.

Tranquility in the Frozen Air

In the stillness, time drifts slow,
A quiet hush, a gentle flow,
Frozen whispers cradle the night,
Tranquility in silver light.

Snowflakes tumble, soft and round,
In this wonder, peace is found,
Each breath a chill, a soft embrace,
As winter weaves its delicate lace.

Stars appear in a velvet sky,
As we wander quietly by,
Our hearts beat in the calm so dear,
Tranquility draws us near.

Footprints fade in the radiant white,
Echoes drift out of sight,
Nature's symphony sings a song,
Where we know that we belong.

In frozen air, true stillness reigns,
As night descends, our souls remain,
Wrapped in cozy winter's hold,
Finding beauty in the cold.

Celestial Snowfall

Underneath a starry dome,
Snowflakes dance, a dreamlike tome,
Celestial whispers fill the night,
A soft descent, a world of light.

Heaven spills its crystal tears,
Filling hearts, dispelling fears,
Every flake a wish set free,
In this moment, you and me.

A blanket white, the landscape glows,
In this hush, the magic flows,
Timeless stories come alive,
In the chill, our spirits thrive.

With every drift, a secret shared,
In winter's grasp, we are ensnared,
Celestial wonders beckon low,
In snowy depths, our love will grow.

The night unfolds, each flake a dream,
In the silence, we are seen,
A timeless dance beneath the sky,
Where celestial snowflakes fly.

Quiet Musings in Snowfall

In a world of white, I pause,
Thoughts dance softly on the breeze,
Snowflakes twirl in silent grace,
Nature whispers through the trees.

Footprints carved in fresh, cold ground,
Memories linger, sweet and bright,
Every flake a story bound,
In the hush of winter's night.

I watch the crystal crystals fall,
Each one unique, a fleeting dream,
A tapestry of silence calls,
Wrapped in winter's gentle seam.

The hush embraces all I see,
A tranquil moment in the air,
In the stillness, I feel free,
Wrapped in warmth, without a care.

The light breaks through, a silver ray,
Painting shadows on the ground,
In this quiet, I'll stay,
Lost in thoughts, so profound.

Fragments of a Winter's Whisper

Beneath a quilt of glistening white,
The world sleeps softly, draped in peace,
Whispers echo in the night,
Winter's spells, a sweet release.

Branches heavy with icy lace,
Crystals shining, pure delight,
A secret song, a frozen trace,
Of love that warms the winter's bite.

With every breath, the air's alive,
A frosty tingle in my lungs,
In this moment, I can thrive,
With echoes of forgotten songs.

Stars above in velvet skies,
Twinkling softly, calm and bright,
In winter's arms, no need for lies,
Each flicker holds a promise tight.

The night wraps round in silver wings,
Dreams take flight on frosted wings,
In this space, my spirit sings,
Winter's grace, the joy it brings.

Frostbitten Fables

Tales of winter softly told,
By the fire's flickering light,
Frostbitten dreams and nights of gold,
Whispers woven with delight.

A hush falls over the dreaming trees,
As the world wraps in a snowy shroud,
Magic dances in the gentle breeze,
Winter's story, whispered loud.

Each flake a word, each drift a line,
In this tome of icy art,
Fables frozen, pure, divine,
Echoes shared from heart to heart.

Beneath the moon's soft, silver glow,
A tale unfolds with every breath,
As shadows stretch and rivers slow,
In the chill, we conquer death.

So gather close and hold the flame,
Let winter's song embrace the night,
In frostbitten fables, call my name,
And weave the threads of shared delight.

Chasing Shadows in the Snow

Footprints fade in white expanse,
Shadows flicker, drift away,
With each glance, I find a chance,
To chase the dusk, the end of day.

The world holds its breath in stillness,
As whispers blend with the cooling air,
I follow echoes, hearts of chillness,
In twilight's grasp, we strip despair.

Fields of snow, like dreams concealed,
Maps that lead to spaces rare,
In the quiet, paths revealed,
Forging bonds that gently care.

Laughter catches in the drift,
Chasing shadows as we run,
In moments shared, our spirits lift,
Dancing like a child in sun.

As daylight slips, the night awakes,
Chasing shadows till they're gone,
In the magic, my heart aches,
With winter's song, I am reborn.

Echoes Beneath the Frost

Silent whispers on the ground,
Thin veils of frost all around.
Nature sleeps with muted breath,
Echoing shadows dance with death.

Crystals gleam in silver light,
Branches heavy, pure and white.
Footsteps lost in frozen dreams,
Wrapped in soft, translucent beams.

The nightingale has found her rest,
Huddled close, she feels the zest.
Moonlight spills on fields of snow,
Calling forth the dreams to flow.

Time stands still beneath the stars,
The world forgotten, behind bars.
Frosty fingers caress the air,
Cradling secrets, soft and rare.

In the stillness, hearts will find,
The echoes of love intertwined.
As nature weaves her silky threads,
We listen close, where silence spreads.

Soft Embrace of Frozen Nights

Underneath the velvet skies,
Softly glistening, winter lies.
With each breath, a cloud of white,
Crafts a beauty in the night.

Gentle flakes begin to fall,
Whispers crashing, nature's call.
Each flake a story, pure and bright,
Carried on the wings of night.

In the calm, the world is hushed,
Every moment sweetly blushed.
Stars above twinkle and wink,
Drawing dreams, as hearts will think.

Wrapped in warmth, we share our gaze,
Lost in winter's quiet maze.
In the soft embrace of night,
Love who knows no bounds of light.

The moon, a guardian so wise,
Guides us through these frozen sighs.
Hand in hand, we face the cold,
Love is worth its weight in gold.

Winter's Lullaby

Hushed and tender, winter sings,
With a melody that brings.
Frosted windows, stories told,
Nature's warmth in bitter cold.

Cradled underneath the stars,
Dreams float softly, near and far.
In the peaceful, silent eves,
Hearts entwined, the world believes.

Snowflakes whirl in gentle dance,
As we dwell in winter's trance.
Every note, a lullaby,
Carried forth on winds that sigh.

In the radiance of the moon,
Whispered secrets linger soon.
Wrapped in love, the fires glow,
In this moment, time is slow.

Winter's song, a soothing balm,
Nestled close, we feel its calm.
With each breath, a promise clear,
Together, we will conquer fear.

Veils of Chill

Misty mornings wrapped in white,
Veils of chill obscure the sight.
Yet within the cold embrace,
Lies a warmth we cannot trace.

Through the trees, a lantern glows,
Guiding paths where silence flows.
Footprints etch a tale unknown,
In a world that feels like home.

Every breath, a puffs of smoke,
Frosty breathe of words we spoke.
In the shadows, glimmers play,
Memories of a brighter day.

As we wander, hearts unite,
In the stillness of the night.
Veils of chill, yet spirits rise,
Together 'neath the starlit skies.

Let the icy winds then blow,
For with love, we surely grow.
In the deepest winter's grasp,
We will bloom; our hearts will clasp.

Shimmering Blanket of White

A soft embrace upon the earth,
Covering all with gentle mirth.
Silver whispers in the night,
Nature sleeps wrapped in white.

Branches bow with heavy load,
Tracks erased on winter's road.
Underneath the quilted glow,
Dreams arise in the deep snow.

Silent streets, a world so still,
Echoes of the frost will thrill.
Stars twinkle in the chilling breeze,
Nights caress like winter's tease.

Footsteps fade, a fleeting trace,
Quiet beauty, a tranquil space.
In this hush, the heart takes flight,
Lost within the velvet white.

Crisp air clings to every breath,
Life awakened, defying death.
In the mirror of the moon's bright,
All is calm, all feels right.

Silent Designs in Winter's Light

Frosted patterns on the glass,
Nature's art does gently pass.
Each twirl and swirl, a crafted dream,
Whispers shared in silver stream.

Frozen streams that softly flow,
Dreams encased beneath the snow.
The sun peeks through, a gentle ray,
Bringing warmth to winter's day.

Birds retreat to cozy nests,
While the cold provides its tests.
Branches lace in winter's thread,
Silent stories left unsaid.

Each snowflake, a world unique,
Delicate, rather than bleak.
They dance like whispers from above,
Winter's beauty, cold yet love.

As twilight paints the sky so fair,
Stars emerge, with frosty flair.
Wrap the night in icy shine,
Winter's magic, so divine.

Glacial Elegy

Mountains rise in icy grace,
Whispered tales of time and space.
Glaciers shimmer in the sun,
Silent giants, battles won.

Ancient ice, a story old,
Tales of warmth and climates cold.
Melting slowly, rivers weep,
Secrets buried, dreams to keep.

Echoes of the past unfold,
Frozen echoes gently told.
Every crack, a silent cry,
Echoing to the distant sky.

Underneath the vast expanse,
Nature's rhythm, a somber dance.
Life unfolds in shades of gray,
As the cold leads hearts astray.

Yet from ice, a promise blooms,
Hope arises from the glooms.
Within the chill, we find the spark,
Glacial songs in winters dark.

Crystal Tapestry of Cold

Threads of frost, so fine and bright,
Woven tales in morning light.
Glistening in each branch and leaf,
A tapestry of cold belief.

Shadows dance on snow's embrace,
Nature paints with gentle grace.
Each crystal drop, a fleeting ghost,
Vanishing, but we can boast.

In gardens where the silence reigns,
Winter whispers through the lanes.
Nature's brush, it sweeps so low,
Covering all with sparkling show.

Underneath the silent dome,
Frozen fields become our home.
Every flake a story spun,
In winter's glow, the journey's begun.

With each breath, the chill we taste,
Time moves slow, we do not haste.
In this crystal, we are held,
A tapestry where dreams are melded.

Dogwood Encased in Crystal

Petals glisten in a frosty light,
Nature's beauty, pure and bright.
Branches heavy, bending low,
In silence, soft the cold winds blow.

A fragile world, a dreamlike sight,
Dogwood blooms in winter's night.
Cascades of ice, like diamonds shine,
In this moment, all feels divine.

Whispers echo through the trees,
Gentle sighs dance with the breeze.
Each droplet captures sun's warm kiss,
A fleeting touch of winter's bliss.

Time stands still beneath this shroud,
Nature wrapped, so soft, so proud.
In crystal prism, colors gleam,
Awakening a slumbered dream.

Beneath the weight of winter's hand,
The dogwood waits, as shadows stand.
A story told in glistening hues,
Of seasons masked in vibrant blues.

Winter's Shimmering Visage

Veils of frost on every tree,
Nature's art, a tapestry.
Sparkling jewels grace the ground,
In silence, beauty's echo sound.

Each flake falls like whispered prayer,
Covering all with tender care.
A crystal sun, so soft and pale,
Illuminates the snowy trail.

Shadows stretch beneath the day,
Winter's spirit finds its way.
Softly glows the evening sky,
As the world begins to sigh.

With every breath, the cold air bites,
Stars emerge in winter nights.
Frosty whispers fill the air,
Enchanting all who linger there.

In this realm, where time is still,
Nature reigns with subtle thrill.
Winter clouds, in silence pass,
On this canvas, dreams amass.

Luminous Veil of Cold

A veil of white, serene and bright,
Covers the world in fragile light.
Every branch, a crystal lace,
Winter's charm, a tranquil face.

Frozen rivers gently gleam,
Reflecting dreams of light supreme.
A hush descends, the night draws near,
In the cold, we hold our dear.

Moonlit whispers dance on snow,
Guiding footsteps, soft and slow.
Each breath visible in the air,
Moments linger, without care.

Beneath the stars, shadows play,
Bathed in warmth of silver ray.
In this silence, hearts align,
Connected by a thread divine.

Winter's glow, a fleeting glance,
Inviting all to join the dance.
A luminous world, where dreams unfold,
Wrapped in winter's tender hold.

Dreamscape of Frosted Fields

Fields adorned in silver sheens,
Nature's quilt of frosty dreams.
Whispers of the morning light,
Painting worlds so soft and bright.

Each blade of grass, a jeweled sight,
Beneath the sun, pure and white.
The air crisp with the scent of pine,
In the stillness, hearts entwine.

Footprints etch the snowy path,
Leading on, a gentle math.
Wandering where the silence sings,
In this land of frosted kings.

Gentle flakes like feathers fall,
Blanketing the world, a call.
Echoing the warmth of dreams,
In this realm where beauty gleams.

Time drifts slowly, whispers flow,
In the magic of winter's glow.
Fields of frost, a canvas wide,
Painting peace where dreams reside.

A Dance Beneath the Icy Glow

Underneath the frosty light,
Whispers of the stars take flight.
Trees adorned in silver lace,
Nature's beauty in this place.

Footprints mark the snowy floor,
Echoes of the night explore.
Moonbeams play a gentle tune,
As shadows dance with light of Moon.

Silent breezes weave a tale,
Of winter's chill, a soft, sweet veil.
Each snowflake drifts down slow,
A magic spell in icy glow.

In the stillness, dreams arise,
Carried on the winter sighs.
Hearts entwined in nature's grace,
A sacred moment we embrace.

Dancing softly, spirits sway,
Lost in night, we drift away.
A world aglow, so vast, so bright,
Beneath this blanket of pure white.

Enchanted Silence of Snowflakes

In the hush of falling white,
Snowflakes dance in soft moonlight.
Each one sparkles, pure and rare,
Whispers float upon the air.

Gentle flakes on every bough,
Nature's quilt, a sacred vow.
Time stands still in this embrace,
Magic roams through every space.

Silhouettes of trees and night,
Wrapped in beauty, pure delight.
The world transforms, a wondrous sight,
Within this calm, hearts feel so light.

Voices hushed, a tranquil scene,
Dreamers lost in forest green.
Together, caught in winter's grace,
In this quiet, we find our place.

Snowflakes twirl, a gentle flight,
Filling hearts with pure delight.
In every flake, a story told,
Of winter's charm, a joy to hold.

Frosty Fables of Yore

In the frost, old tales arise,
From the earth to endless skies.
Wind whispers secrets of the past,
As winter's chill holds fast.

Once upon a time they say,
Magic ruled both night and day.
With every flake that fell from high,
Legends soared into the sky.

Creatures wandered, stories spun,
In the glow of setting sun.
Fables danced on icy streams,
Carried forth on winter dreams.

Elders spoke of ancient lore,
In the warmth, they would explore.
Gathered close beside the fire,
Echoing tales that never tire.

Frosted windows, patterns grand,
Every detail is carefully planned.
Tales of old come alive once more,
In the heart of winter's core.

Veil of Frosted Twilight

Twilight softens, light retreats,
Draped in frost, the world completes.
A velvet touch on every lane,
Silence cloaked in gentle rain.

Stars awaken, skies aglow,
Underneath this frozen show.
Nighttime whispers, secrets share,
In the hush, we find our prayer.

Misty breaths in cold embrace,
Nature's wonders, timeless grace.
In the veil of twilight's hold,
Stories of the night unfold.

Dances linger in the air,
Frosted wonders everywhere.
The moonlight serenades the trees,
Carrying soft, enchanted pleas.

Each moment wrapped in sweet delight,
In this realm of frosted night.
Veiled in dreams, the world is still,
As winter weaves its gentle thrill.

The Silvered Silence

In the twilight glow so fair,
Whispers float upon the air.
Moonlight dances on the ground,
In the stillness, peace is found.

Stars entwined in the vast sky,
Dreams awaken, soft and shy.
Every heartbeat, every sigh,
Echoes gently, drifting by.

Beneath a veil of silver light,
Hope ignites the endless night.
Flickering shadows start to play,
Guiding hearts along the way.

Silence hums a tender song,
Drawing souls to where they belong.
In this moment, time stands still,
Wrapped in warmth, a subtle thrill.

Journey forth with open eyes,
Through the quiet, where love lies.
In the silvered silence here,
Find the strength to face your fear.

Veil of Eternal Winter

In the realm of endless night,
Frozen hearts in soft moonlight.
Snowflakes whisper, secrets old,
Wrapped in blankets, pale and cold.

Every branch, a crystal crown,
Silent majesty weighs down.
Footprints lost in drifting snow,
Time is frozen, still and slow.

Fires flicker with a sigh,
Heating dreams that dare to fly.
In the stillness, memories gleam,
Carried forth on winter's dream.

Veils of frost, they softly fall,
Holding secrets, nature's call.
In this solitude, we learn,
That the fires of love still burn.

Underneath the icy sheen,
Lies a warmth, though seldom seen.
Through the cold, our spirits rise,
Breaking through the winter skies.

Glistening Shadows

Beneath the trees, the shadows play,
As evening melts to shades of gray.
Moonbeams scatter, gentle light,
Painting dreams in softest night.

Glistening paths of silver sheen,
Lead us through this tranquil scene.
Each turn hides a secret kept,
In the silence, love has leapt.

Branches weave a delicate song,
Telling tales of where we belong.
In the glimmer, hope is found,
Whispers echo all around.

Every heartbeat, every glance,
Draws us deeper into chance.
In the shadows, light will splash,
Guiding us through shadows' clash.

With every step, the world unfolds,
In these glistening tales retold.
Hand in hand, we chase the light,
Through the shadows, into night.

Hushed Beneath the Snow

Hushed beneath the quilt of white,
Every sound, a soft delight.
Winter's breath, a gentle kiss,
Whispers hold a frosted bliss.

Frosted trees stand tall and proud,
Veiling secrets, soft and loud.
In their shadows, dreams take flight,
Guiding souls through frozen night.

This stillness cradles every tear,
Find the warmth when paths are clear.
Through the cold, our spirits soar,
In the quiet, we explore.

Snowflakes fall like tender words,
Filling silence, softly heard.
In the hush, we come alive,
With each heartbeat, we survive.

Wrapped in dreams of white and gray,
Embracing winter's soft display.
Hushed beneath this frozen glow,
Together we will learn to grow.

Snowy Lattice of Time

Frosted branches bend with grace,
Nature's quilt on the ground,
Each flake drifting, soft in pace,
Caught in time, without a sound.

Whispers echo in the night,
Stars peer through the silken veil,
Memories dance in silver light,
As the world begins to pale.

Footsteps crunch, a moment's tune,
Echoes lost in winter's breath,
Moonlit shadows hum a rune,
Marking paths of life and death.

Every flake a story told,
Fleeting moments, crystals bright,
With every fold the past unfolds,
Embraced in the arms of night.

In this stillness, truth awaits,
Wrapped in layers, pure and free,
Snowy lattice weaves our fates,
Bound together, you and me.

Shining Whispers of a Frozen Dawn

When night gives way to light's embrace,
The world awakes, a gentle sigh,
Gold and silver fill the space,
As daybreak paints the frosty sky.

Softly glowing, shadows dance,
Whispers flicker on the breeze,
A frozen moment's sweet romance,
Wrapped in warmth, the heart's unease.

Time stands still in this bright glow,
Every breath an echo's song,
In this silence, feelings flow,
Where the shy and brave belong.

Glistening paths of melting snow,
Invite the dawn to take a chance,
In shining whispers, secrets grow,
As day unfolds in a frosty trance.

Together we can take the leap,
Into the warmth of morning's hue,
Where dreams awaken from their sleep,
And frozen hearts, begin anew.

Gossamer Threads in a Winter's Web

Delicate strands of icy lace,
Woven through the trees and air,
Each thread tells a timeless tale,
Of winter's breath, both wild and rare.

Crystal droplets catch the light,
Sparkling like a thousand stars,
In the hush of fading night,
Nature weaves its endless bars.

Tangled branches intertwine,
In a dance both bold and meek,
A tapestry, pure, divine,
Whispers of the softest speak.

Gossamer dreams float gently down,
Adrift upon the chilly breeze,
In their beauty, they astound,
Crafted with such tender ease.

Life's own web, both fierce and fine,
Holds moments precious and profound,
In winter's grasp, we intertwine,
Finding warmth where love is found.

Veil of White Softly Falling

A cloak of white drapes the earth,
Softly falling, pure and slow,
Each flake, a whispered rebirth,
In winter's pulse, a gentle flow.

Blankets wrap the silent ground,
Crystals catch the morning light,
All around, the world unbound,
As magic drapes the scene so bright.

Footsteps fade in snowy dreams,
Lost within this chilly grace,
Nature's peace, or so it seems,
In the hush, we find our place.

Veils entwine in pure delight,
Wrapping moments, still and close,
In this quiet, hearts unite,
Underneath the snowy rose.

Let the world outside stand still,
As soft flakes weave soft memories,
In the magic, feel the thrill,
Of winter's sweet harmonies.

Ethereal Drift of Flurries

A dance of snowflakes, light and free,
They swirl through the air, a soft decree.
Each gentle touch, a lover's kiss,
In winter's breath, a fleeting bliss.

The world transforms, a canvas white,
Where shadows merge with the soft twilight.
Beneath the sky, a hush descends,
As time stands still, the cold extends.

Footprints linger, then fade away,
Lost in the dream of the snow's ballet.
Branches bow down, heavy with cheer,
In quiet moments, the magic's near.

Drifting softly, the flakes unite,
A tapestry woven with pure delight.
In every flurry, whispers abound,
Nature's secrets in silence found.

Night unfolds, stars blink awake,
In this frost-hued world, my heart does shake.
For in the drift of flurries fine,
Lies the essence of the divine.

Frostbitten Silence

The world wrapped tight in winter's grasp,
Where echoes of laughter seem to rasp.
Silent whispers in the frostbite air,
Each breath a cloud, a moment rare.

Icicles hang like ancient swords,
Glistening sharp in the sun's rewards.
The ground is hard, a frozen song,
In this stillness, we all belong.

Winter's embrace, a cold caress,
Leaves the landscape in icy dress.
With every step, the crunch resounds,
In this frozen world, peace abounds.

Trees stand tall, their branches bare,
Guardians of secrets layered and rare.
In the shivering air, a beauty stark,
In frostbitten silence, a whispered spark.

Beneath the chill, a warmth does hide,
Waiting to bloom, winter's pride.
So let the stillness softly stay,
As hearts find warmth in the cold ballet.

Whispered Secrets Beneath the Ice

Beneath the surface, stories sleep,
In crystal chambers, dark and deep.
The secrets kept from light's embrace,
In icy realms, a hidden place.

Whispers travel through the frozen ground,
Echoes of life that once were found.
Fractured memories, a fleeting glance,
In the silence, they twirl and dance.

Winter's breath holds the tales so tight,
Of summer's warmth and autumn's flight.
Each slumbering whisper, a silent plea,
A promise of spring, of life set free.

Glistening frost like enchanted lace,
Veils the secrets in nature's grace.
From earth to sky, the story flows,
In whispered secrets, the magic grows.

And as the thaw begins to creep,
From shadows cold, the stories leap.
With every drop, the life returns,
In whispered secrets, the heart still yearns.

Shrouded Paths of a Winter's Tale

In twilight's grasp, the paths unwind,
With whispers soft, the trees aligned.
Each step is careful, each breath a sigh,
In shrouded walks where shadows lie.

The air is crisp, as time moves slow,
Footsteps cause a gentle snow.
A world transformed, a dream in white,
In winter's arms, the heart takes flight.

Through tangled woods where silence reigns,
A hidden beauty, the cold contains.
Beneath the boughs, the secrets grow,
In frozen tales of ice and snow.

Stars reflect on the icy lake,
Guiding the dreamers, the paths they take.
With every turn, a mystery waits,
In shrouded paths, the soul relates.

And as the dawn breaks, a gold embrace,
The paths will melt, but not erase.
For in the memories, the story'll dwell,
On shrouded paths of a winter's tale.

Enchanted by the Chill

A whisper of frost in the evening air,
The world adorned in glistening white,
Trees draped in silver, a moment so rare,
Beneath the stars, the heart takes flight.

Echoes of laughter dance through the night,
Children bundled, joy in their play,
Snowflakes twirling, a magical sight,
In this winter wonderland, we stay.

Candles flicker in cozy retreat,
With cocoa steaming, warmth in our hands,
The chill outside feels soft and sweet,
As fire crackles and gently reprimands.

Footprints lead through the slumbering pines,
Nature's blanket, a calming embrace,
Each breath a poem that softly defines,
The beauty of winter, a tranquil pace.

With every flake, a moment's delight,
A dance of the season, enchanting and bright,
In chilled serenity, we find our peace,
As the world wraps us in winter's fleece.

Lullabies of the Snowstorm

Snowflakes falling, a soft lullaby,
The wind whispers secrets, a gentle sigh,
Night blankets earth in a silvery glow,
Harmonies weave where the cold winds blow.

Candles flicker in the still of the hour,
Wrapped in a quilt, some read flowers,
The beauty of silence, a moment serene,
In whispers of snow, life feels like a dream.

Trees bow down with their frosted crowns,
The world transformed in crystalline gowns,
Each flake a note in a symphonic sound,
While the snowfall dances and spins all around.

Fires crackle like woodlands awake,
A warmth that envelops, a soothing take,
Moments of peace, in the storm we find,
The lullabies of winter, so sweet and kind.

As night deepens, we drift into sleep,
Dreams painted white, in silence we keep,
The snowstorm sings as it covers the land,
In its tender embrace, together we stand.

When the World Turns Soft

When the world turns soft and hues fade away,
A blanket of white, the colors lay low,
The chill in the air whispers stories of play,
And memories spark in the glow of the snow.

Every step taken leaves traces behind,
Laughter of children, a symphony sweet,
The softness of winter, a calm for the mind,
In cottony dreams where the world feels complete.

Stars peek through clouds, like gems in the night,
While branches are laden, a delicate sight,
The winds gently carry the secrets of old,
As hearts gather close, feeling warm and bold.

With tea brewed to hold and stories to share,
Beside glowing embers, the fire's embrace,
When the world turns soft, we find time to care,
Connecting our hearts in this magical place.

So let the night linger, let the silence fall,
In the depth of the winter, we'll heed the call,
As dreams intertwine, and our spirits rise,
In the soft of the world, we find paradise.

Frosted Serenity

In the hush of the morning, soft whispers arise,
A canvas of frost under clear, azure skies,
Nature adorned in a pearl-studded dress,
Each flake a reminder, a moment to bless.

Birds flit and flutter, their breath visible,
Painting the air with a presence so lyrical,
The world gently waking from slumber's embrace,
In the frosted serenity, beauty finds grace.

Sunrise peeks shyly, casting gold on the snow,
Transforming the stillness in a radiant glow,
Each tree stands a witness to time softly passing,
As nature's orchestra plays, ever contrasting.

The whispers of winter, a soothing refrain,
Will echo in hearts, like a warm soothing rain,
In moments of peace, find the stillness inside,
In frosted serenity, let your spirit glide.

With hearts wide open, we greet the day bright,
Wrapped in the magic of winter's soft light,
In the quiet of nature, our souls intertwine,
In the beauty of stillness, forever we shine.

Glacial Murmurs

In silence deep, the glaciers sigh,
Whispers of ages, as time drifts by.
Cracks and creaks tell tales untold,
Frozen secrets, in ice enfold.

Shimmering blue in a world of white,
Dancing shadows in the moonlit night.
Each breath of wind, a soft lament,
Glacial murmurs, a heart's content.

Reflections flicker on crystal shores,
Nature's canvas, forever endows.
An art of frost, both cruel and kind,
In every flake, a story confined.

As daylight fades, the horizon glows,
Colors awaken, a symphony grows.
The glacial breath, both stark and clear,
Echoes of life, for those who hear.

In mountain's grasp, the silence reigns,
Eternal beauty, in stillness gains.
A world untouched, where few can tread,
In glacial murmurs, our hearts are led.

The Frosted Artist's Canvas

Upon a morn, the world adorned,
With frosted whispers, magic born.
Each tree embraced by winter's hand,
A canvas bright across the land.

Brush strokes of white on every bough,
Nature's art, we humbly bow.
Glistening jewels on branches sway,
A wondrous sight, a bright display.

The sky draped low, a muted hue,
With every flake, a tale anew.
In every corner, beauty thrives,
The artist's touch, where silence dives.

Footprints trace a gentle path,
In patterns soft, away from wrath.
Children laugh in the chilly glow,
Creating scenes like falling snow.

As daylight wanes, the colors shift,
From bright to dusk, a graceful lift.
Under the stars, the canvas gleams,
In frosted whispers, the night redeems.

A Tapestry of Icy Luster

Woven threads of silver light,
Spin a tapestry, pure and bright.
Each icy strand, a story spun,
In winter's grasp, where dreams run.

Frost-kissed leaves in patterns dance,
Nature's rhythm, a fleeting chance.
Crystalline lace upon the ground,
With every step, enchantment found.

Ridges sharp, and valleys deep,
Where whispers of the winter creep.
Glistening pathways beckon near,
A quiet world where hearts may steer.

Beneath the stars, the canvas glows,
An evening's hush, the magic flows.
Each breath of air, a chill, a thrill,
In icy beauty, the senses fill.

A tapestry of frosty dreams,
In winter's heart, where silence beams.
Bound by luster, forever cast,
In whispers soft, our souls are amassed.

Secrets Wrapped in White

Beneath the veil of winter's grace,
Lies a world, a quiet space.
Secrets wrapped in blankets white,
Hushed like stars, in velvet night.

The frosty breath of silent trees,
Carries stories on the breeze.
Each twirl of snow, a lost embrace,
Echoes of time, a gentle trace.

In shadows deep, where whispers play,
Hide mysteries of yesterday.
Crystal reflections, soft and bright,
Guarded tales in the pale moonlight.

Every flake, a fragile spell,
Marking pathways, where few dwell.
In this calm, our hearts align,
Wrapped in secrets, pure, divine.

When spring awakes, the ice will break,
Yet till then, the dreams will wake.
In frosted silence, truths reside,
Wrapped in white, the world abides.

Frost-kissed Memories

In the autumn's fading light,
Whispers of the past take flight.
Footsteps crunch on frozen ground,
Echoes of laughter all around.

Each flake falls like a silent tear,
Kissed by frost, memories clear.
Time stands still, a fleeting glance,
In the moment, we find our chance.

Windows fogged with childhood dreams,
Softening the world's harsh seams.
We gather 'round the fire's glow,
Sharing secrets we once know.

With every sigh, the evening sighs,
Frosted, soft, beneath the skies.
In the chill, we find our warmth,
Wrapped in stories, love's true form.

As shadows stretch and daylight fades,
We weave our lives in nature's glades.
A tapestry of heart and soul,
Together we make each other whole.

A Canvas of Icy Wonder

Nature drapes in white array,
Each branch dressed, a stunning display.
Frozen breath, the world does gleam,
A canvas of beauty, like a dream.

Dancing lights in the frosty air,
Every flake, a brushstroke rare.
Crystals twinkle on the ground,
In this wonder, peace abounds.

Mountains stand, serene and bold,
Stories whispered, yet untold.
Snowflakes flutter from the skies,
A magic that never dies.

Echoing laughter through the trees,
Chill and warmth held in a breeze.
A world transformed, pure delight,
Beneath the soft, enchanting light.

With each step, the heart ignites,
Boundless joy on winter nights.
In this realm, we roam and play,
A canvas painted with yesterday.

Gleaming Silence at Dusk

As the sun dips down low,
Silence wraps the world in snow.
Shadows dance, twilight stands,
Beauty woven by nature's hands.

Each glimmer holds a secret path,
In the quiet, we find our math.
Stars awaken, one by one,
Whispers of the day now done.

A blanket soft cradles the land,
Peace enfolds like a gentle hand.
The twilight hums a soothing tune,
Underneath the watchful moon.

Glistening trees like silver crowns,
In the stillness, time unwounds.
Each breath taken feels divine,
In the gleamisht silence, we intertwine.

Dreams take flight on winter's breath,
In the dusk, we dance with death.
Yet hope flickers, soft and bright,
Gleaming silence, pure delight.

Twinkling Stars on a Frozen Sky

Beneath a canvas, dark and deep,
Twinkling stars, secrets they keep.
Frozen air, a magic theme,
Each light dances, a soft gleam.

Whispers of far-off places call,
In the night, we feel so small.
Constellations guide our heart,
Infinite, a work of art.

Snowflakes sprinkle the ground below,
Mirroring the celestial show.
With every breath, a story starts,
In the silence, we find our parts.

Underneath this starry dome,
We find solace, a gentle home.
Each twinkle draws us near,
In frozen wonder, without fear.

As we gaze at the frozen light,
Dreams take flight into the night.
Together, hearts and spirits fly,
Twinkling stars on a frozen sky.

Serene Solitude in Hibernation

In winter's grasp, the world stands still,
A blanket white upon the hill.
Silent whispers in the frosty air,
Nature's pause, so pure and rare.

Underneath the shimmering snow,
Life awaits, in dreams they glow.
Cradled softly, time abides,
In this peace, the heart resides.

Moonlit nights bring stars so bright,
Casting shadows, a tranquil sight.
Lost in thoughts, both deep and wide,
Serene solitude, my faithful guide.

The world outside, a distant sound,
In hibernation, solace found.
Embraced by the chill, yet warm within,
Awakening dreams, where hope begins.

With every breath, the silence sings,
In winter's clutch, the spirit clings.
As frost-kissed leaves begin to fade,
New life will bloom, unafraid.

Glistening Horizon of a Snowy Dream

The sun arises, bright and bold,
Casting gems on snow like gold.
A horizon glistens, pure and bright,
A canvas painted with morning light.

Clouds dance softly in the breeze,
Whispers carried through the trees.
Each flake descending, a gentle sigh,
Kissing earth as it floats nigh.

Footsteps crunch on the frosty floor,
Every step reveals something more.
The snowy dream, a world anew,
Unraveled wonders, just for you.

The mountains stand, their peaks adorned,
In jeweled splendor, nature's scorned.
Yet in this beauty, peace resides,
A glistening horizon where joy abides.

With every glimmer, hope is found,
In the icy hush, our hearts unbound.
Dreams take flight on winter's wing,
In a world of white, our spirits sing.

Quiet Reflections in White

The quiet whispers of a snowy morn,
Where gentle silence is reborn.
Trees draped in white, a still embrace,
Each flake a story of nature's grace.

Footprints lingering, fading slow,
Tales untold within the snow.
Reflections dance in icy streams,
In the calm, we find our dreams.

Beneath the surface, life persists,
In quiet pools, the world exists.
Mirrored skies in crystalline,
Every moment, a true divine.

The frosty breath of winter's chill,
Wraps around, so subtle, still.
In this white, our hearts unite,
Finding solace in the night.

With every glance, new wonder grows,
In quiet reflections, peace bestows.
The snowflakes fall, soft and light,
In perfect harmony, day and night.

Icebound Chronicles

In icy realms where stories sleep,
Frozen whispers, secrets deep.
Each crystal tells of days long past,
Chronicles etched in winter's grasp.

Beneath the frost, the earth lies still,
Hopes and dreams await the thrill.
Silent echoes through the trees,
Softly carried by the breeze.

The winds of change will soon arrive,
Awakening life, keeping it alive.
In these chronicles of ice and snow,
Nature's tapestry begins to flow.

Mysterious paths in the frozen land,
Every step, a story planned.
In marrow cold, yet warm with light,
Icebound chronicles, pure delight.

Awash in hues of blue and white,
The heart finds peace in winter's night.
From frozen dreams, new tales ascend,
In icebound chronicles, time won't end.

Secrets Beneath the Frost

In the stillness of the night,
Where shadows softly creep,
The frost conceals what lies below,
Old secrets, buried deep.

Beneath the icy, glimmering veil,
Whispers of time do stay,
Ancient tales of love and loss,
Silenced by winter's sway.

Leaves that once danced in the sun,
Now frozen in their plight,
But listen close, you'll hear their song,
Echoes in the quiet light.

Silent oaths beneath the chill,
Promises only earth can keep,
The frost, a guardian of dreams,
Cradles secrets in its sleep.

A world transformed, a canvas white,
Where magic weaves its sheer delight,
Beneath the frost, life waits anew,
In whispers soft and true.

Wrapped in Winter's Whisper

The world is wrapped in blankets white,
A hush falls on the frozen ground,
Every breath a cloud of mist,
In winter's quiet, peace is found.

Trees stand tall with coats of snow,
Their limbs embrace the gentle frost,
While whispers float on icy winds,
Tales of warmth that never lost.

Stars above twinkle like diamonds,
In the deep velvet of night's embrace,
Each flicker a promise of hope,
Shining in the silent space.

Fireplaces crackle softly now,
Embers dance in the cozy glow,
While outside the world wears a crown,
Of shimmering crystals in tow.

So let us hold this moment close,
Wrapped in winter's gentle breath,
For every whisper carried forth,
Is life that flourishes from death.

Whispers of Winter's Shroud

In the heart of winter's shroud,
Soft voices whisper low,
Through branches bare and fields of white,
They share the tales of snow.

A blanket soft upon the earth,
Hides colors once so bright,
Yet in the stillness, life persists,
Hidden from our sight.

The chill wraps round like a gentle kiss,
A reminder of the past,
That even in the coldest nights,
All things cannot last.

Frozen rivers, silent dreams,
Flow beneath the ice,
With every shimmer, every gleam,
The world thinks twice.

So let the whispers guide us home,
Through valleys wrapped in frost,
For in their secrets, we shall find,
The warmth we thought was lost.

Frosted Dreams on Silent Streets

The streets are hushed, a soft embrace,
As winter paints the town,
With frosted dreams that sparkle bright,
In patches all around.

Footprints lead through glistening lanes,
Where laughter once rang clear,
Now echoing in silent nights,
And memories are near.

Streetlamps glow like distant stars,
Shrouded gently in white,
They softly guide the wandering souls,
Through winter's calm delight.

Underneath the blanket cold,
Life holds its breath in peace,
As frost-kissed dreams whisper low,
Hoping not to cease.

Beneath the twinkle of the night,
Every heart seeks warmth anew,
In the quiet of the frosted streets,
We find a world so true.

A Glimmer Beneath the Drift

The soft snow whispers on the ground,
A hidden spark, a secret found.
Underneath, the earth does breathe,
Life awakes, beneath the wreath.

Beneath the weight of winter's grace,
A tiny light begins to trace.
Every flake a tale to tell,
In silence, all is woven well.

Glimmers dance in chilly air,
A world untouched, a moment rare.
The heavens watch with twinkling eyes,
As shadows blend with twilight skies.

The drifts may hide, but dreams remain,
Each glimmer holds the promise plain.
With every chill, a warmth will grow,
Awakening life from depths of snow.

As spring approaches, murmurs rise,
The sun will break through cloudy skies.
A glimmer here, a touch of light,
Beneath the drift, hope shines so bright.

Shrouded in Crystal Light

A world enfolded in icy beams,
Where every corner softly gleams.
Shadows cast in gentle hues,
Whisper secrets nature views.

The forest wears a frosted crown,
In crystal light, it won't back down.
Each branch a prism, caught in time,
With every flicker, sings a rhyme.

Snowflakes fall like whispered prayers,
Upon the ground, a stillness shares.
In this slumber, peace abides,
Wrapped in warmth, where beauty hides.

A breeze arrives, a fleeting touch,
Each breath holds everyone's heart much.
A tranquil space amidst the chill,
In crystal light, the world stands still.

Through winter's heart, the whispers flow,
Each shimmering flake, a tale to sow.
In echoes soft, the stories fade,
Shrouded in light, the dreams cascade.

Frostbite and Gossamer

In twilight's grasp, the cold winds sigh,
Frostbite lingers, as shadows fly.
Gossamer threads weave through the night,
A fragile dance in fading light.

The world transforms, a silken sheen,
Where each breath creates a ghostly scene.
The biting chill reveals its grace,
In quiet wonders, a soft embrace.

With every step, the crunch resounds,
In frozen realms, stillness abounds.
The heartbeats quicken, spirits soar,
Through frosty landscapes, we explore.

A tapestry of silver dreams,
Where moonlight flows and starlight gleams.
The night holds secrets, pure and bright,
In frost and gossamer, pure delight.

Yet as dawn breaks, the chill must fade,
Revealing warmth in autumn's shade.
Frostbite whispers of days long past,
While gossamer memories forever last.

Beneath the Winter's Cloak

Beneath the cloak of winter's chill,
The earth lies quiet, the air is still.
In dreamy white, the world concealed,
A hidden warmth remains unrevealed.

Snowflakes fall like whispered wishes,
Each one carries dreams and kisses.
They blanket fields in purest white,
While stars above shine through the night.

The branches bow beneath their load,
A testament to the paths we've strode.
In frozen moments, time stands tall,
As nature hears the winter's call.

Yet spring will come to break the spell,
Beneath the cloak, life will compel.
Colors burst as warmth returns,
Within the heart, a spark still burns.

So let the snow fall where it may,
Beneath the cloak, we find our way.
In every drift, a dream will bloom,
As winter gives way to spring's perfume.

Milton Keynes UK
Ingram Content Group UK Ltd.
UKHW010228111224
452348UK00011B/579